The ABCs of HBCUs

COLORING BOOK

WORDS BY

CLAUDIA WALKER

PICTURES BY

WHIMSICAL DESIGNS BY CJ

The ABCs of HBCUs Coloring Book
Copyright © 2021 Claudia Walker

ISBN: 978-1-7356435-2-6

All rights reserved. No part of this book may be reproduced or used in any manner without the prior written permission of the copyright owner, except for the use of brief quotations in a book review.

Words and Concepts by: Claudia Walker
Pictures by: Whimsical Designs by CJ
Cover Art by: Jessica E. Boyd

Published by:
HBCU Prep School, LLC.
Oakland, CA

https://hbcuprepschool.com

Printed in China

A is for African-American Studies

B is for Battle of the Bands

C is for Computer Coding Classes

D is for Decision Day

E is for Engineering Excellence

F is for Fraternity brothers

G is for Generations of Graduates

H is for Homecoming

I is for Illustrious Institutions

J is for Judges seeking Justice

K is for Knowledge is King

L is for "Lift Every Voice and Sing"

M is for Motivated Medical students

N is for Never-ending Network

O is for Original safe space

P is for Prolific Professors

Q is for Quintessential campus Queens

R is for Roommates

S is for Sorority Sisters

T is for Time-honored Traditions

U is for Undaunted Undergraduates

V is for Visionaries

Rosa Parks attended Alabama State University's Laboratory High School.

W is for "Why We love our HBCUs"

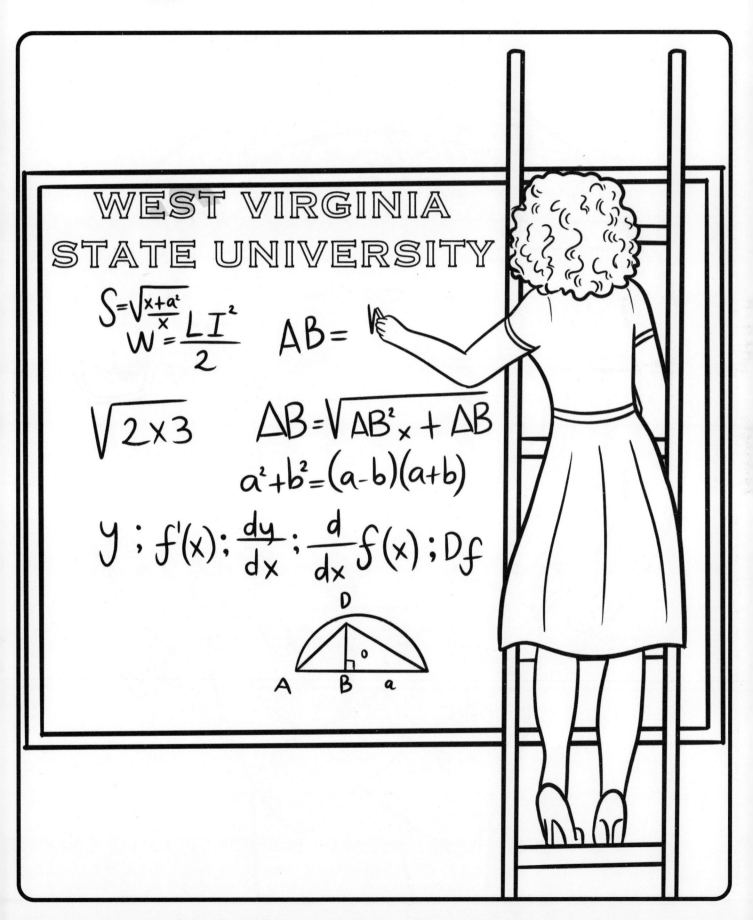

X is for X-factor

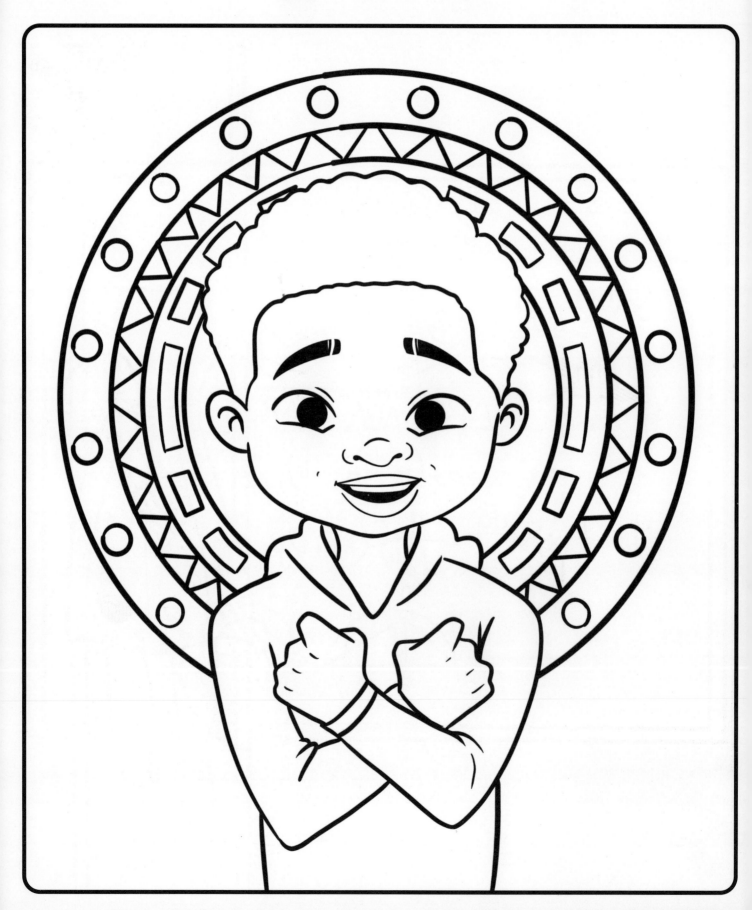

X is for X-factor

Y is for Young, Gifted and Black

Z is for Zora Neale Hurston

I am talented.

My future is bright!

Morris Brown College is in Atlanta, Georgia.

Claflin University is in Orangeburg, South Carolina.

Game time at Tougaloo College!

St. Augustine's University launched the first HBCU cycling team.

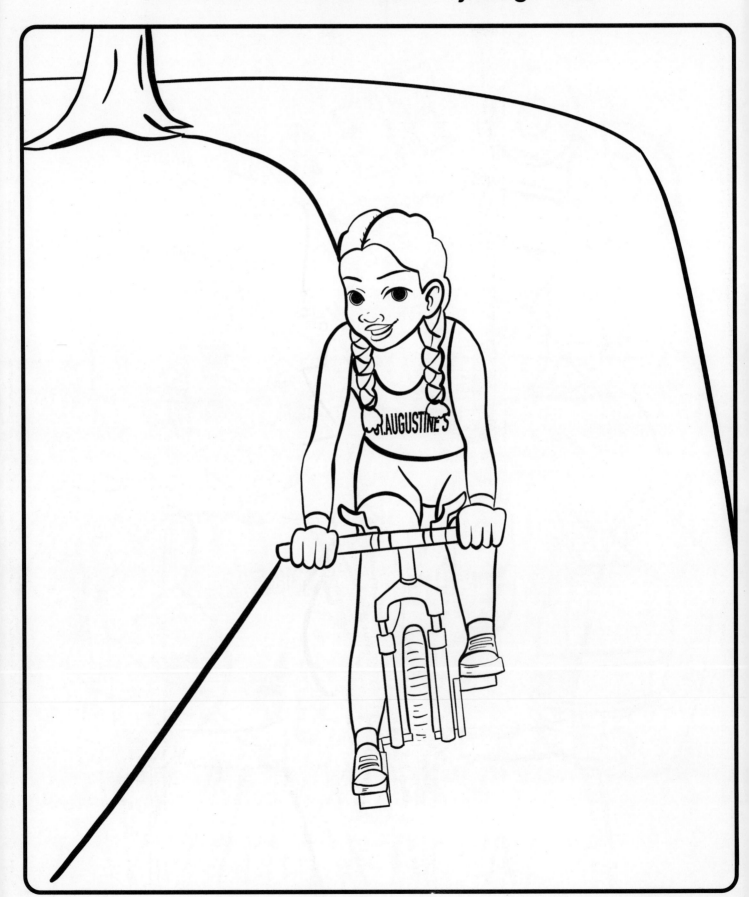

Lincoln University of Missouri was founded in 1866 by African-American soldiers.

Alabama has more HBCUs than any other state!

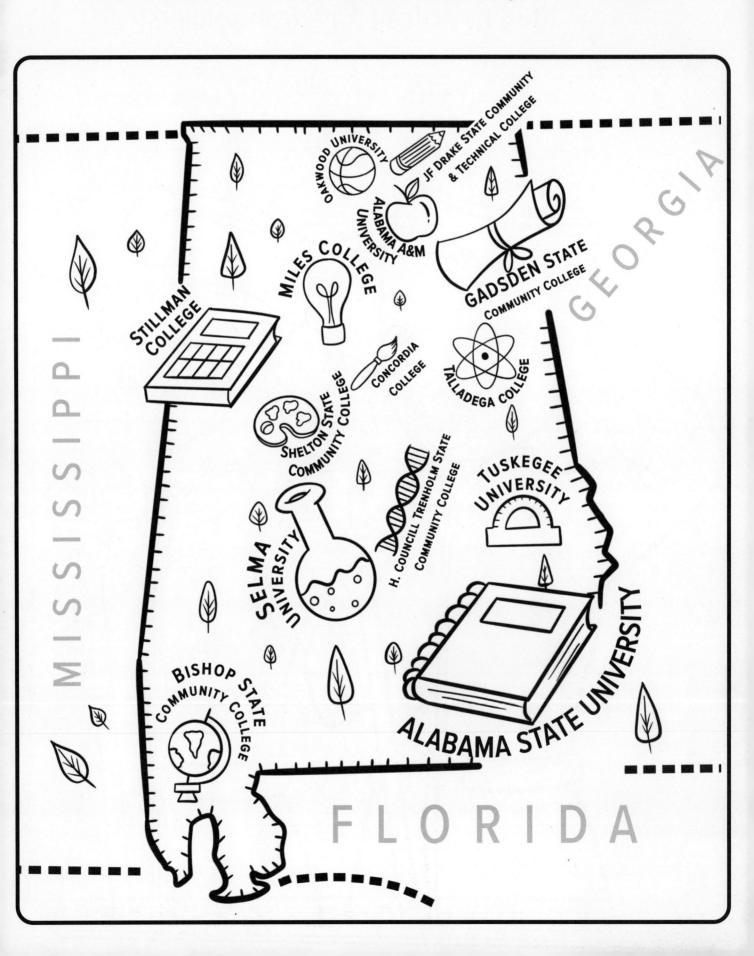

List of HBCUs in Alabama

1. Alabama A&M University
2. Alabama State University
3. Bishop State Community College
4. Concordia College
5. Gadsden State Community College
6. H. Councill Trenholm State Community College
7. JF Drake State Community & Technical College
8. Miles College
9. Oakwood University
10. Selma University
11. Shelton State Community College
12. Stillman College
13. Talladega College
14. Tuskegee University

Do you like animals?

4 HBCUs have Veterinary programs: **Delaware State, FAMU, Fort Valley State,** and **Tuskegee University.**

Future astronauts can study Aerospace at the University of Maryland Eastern Shore, Florida Memorial, and Tennessee State University.

What's the weather in your neighborhood?

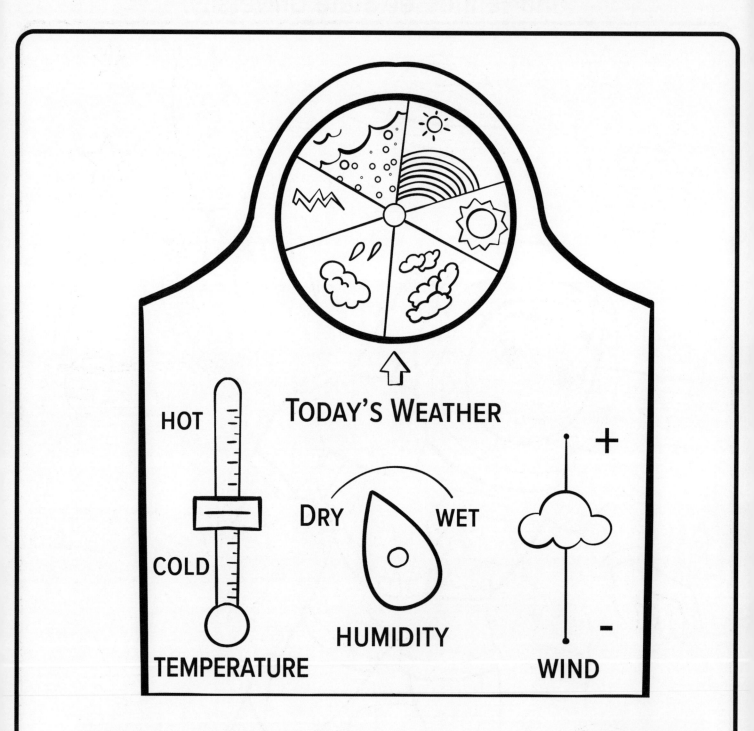

A Meteorologist helps us understand the weather. **Howard, Hampton, North Carolina A&T,** and **Jackson State** have great Meteorology programs.

Learn to become a Firefighter at...

Albany State University, **Fayetteville State University**, and **University of the District of Columbia**.

What's your favorite food?

Denmark Technical, Lawson State, and **St. Philip's College** have Culinary Arts programs.

Many HBCUs, like the ones below, are connected to the Christian church.

Allen, American Baptist, Arkansas Baptist, Barber-Scotia, Birmingham-Easonian, Edward Waters, Hood, Jarvis Christian, LeMoyne-Owen, Morris, Simmons College of Kentucky, and **Virginia University of Lynchburg**

HBCU kids (and their parents) are always stylish!

Clark Atlanta, Cheyney, Hinds and **Coahoma State** have great Fashion Design programs.

You can study Dance at **Coppin State**, **Howard**, and **Johnson C. Smith**.

I'm HBCU Bound!